W9-CXL-125

It's OK
Not To Be OK®
During a Crisis

It's OK
Not To Be OK®
_D_uring a Crisis

How to Live Through and Overcome Adversity

MARK D. LERNER, PH.D.

MARK LERNER ASSOCIATES, INC.
NEW YORK

Published by Mark Lerner Associates, Inc.

It's OK Not To Be OK® *During a Crisis,*
How to Live Through and Overcome Adversity
© 2008 by Mark D. Lerner, Ph.D.

All rights reserved. Printed in the United States of America. No part of this book may be used or reproduced in any manner whatsoever without written permission of the author.

This book is intended solely for informational and educational purposes and not as medical or psychological advice. If you have questions or concerns regarding your health, please consult with your health care provider.

FIRST EDITION

Mark Lerner Associates, Inc. Publications
P.O. Box 1315
Melville, N.Y. 11747

MarkLernerAssociates.org
Tel. (631) 673-3513

Library of Congress Control Number: 2008904165

ISBN 978-0-9772818-2-4

Original pastel and jacket design by Julia Lerner
JuliaLerner.com

Dedicated to You

*May this book help you to live through adversity today
and find new meaning and a new sense of purpose
in your life tomorrow.*

Contents

Appendices

Introduction

"Everything will be okay. It's going to take time...."

But it's not okay now. You've been grappling with intense feelings of aloneness, anxiety, anger, sadness and fear. Sometimes things don't seem real.

While there are books that can help you, they arrive with way too much information, too late. *What about now?* What can ease your emotional pain and keep you functioning *during* this difficult time?

This little book will empower you to understand what's happening to you as you navigate through the rough waters of this storm. It will answer your questions and guide you with practical coping strategies. It will give you hope.

I know that you've been hurting and I understand that it's hard to concentrate. That's precisely why the messages that follow are brief and to the point. Read just one or two at a time. Reflect on how they apply to you, then come back and read a few more when you're ready.

I'm going to help you to harness the painful energy inside you, and use that energy to empower you to live through and overcome this adversity.

1.
It's OK Not To Be OK

The tragic loss of someone special in your life. An illness or injury. A relationship problem. Divorce. Physical or sexual abuse. A work-related crisis. An accident. Criminal victimization. War. A disaster....

What's happening in your life?

During a crisis, when you find yourself struggling to function and it feels like your whole world has changed, *it's okay not to be okay.*

As human beings, we're built to survive. We have inborn mechanisms that help us to recover and heal from the overwhelming challenges that we face during our lifetime. Yet we experience so many normal reactions during a crisis: We're anxious and scared. It's difficult for us to focus and make decisions. It's hard to turn off the painful tape of what's happened. We're excessively watchful and cautious. We're startled by every loud noise. We withdraw from people. We experience headaches and body aches. We have difficulty sleeping. We're disturbed by dreams. We may question our faith. The list goes on.

Am I talking about you? Please, stay with me.

During a crisis, we experience *normal* reactions in the face of an *abnormal* event and *it's okay not to be okay.*

2.
How You Respond ...
It's Your Choice

You're reading this book in the wake of a loss in your life. Whether it's the loss of a special person or people, the loss of a physical ability, loss of your health, loss of your possessions, or the loss of a familiar way of life, you're grieving.

Loss is what's happened to you. Grieving is the normal process that you're going through—your journey of healing. This isn't a passive experience. You don't have to sit back and suffer alone. As much as you're hurting, *you have the ability to choose how you'll respond to your loss. And your response will have a profound affect on how you feel and how you function.*

While we have little control over the events that occur in the world around us, we have tremendous control of our thoughts and what we choose to do. You've chosen to read this book, so there's a part of you that's already committed to overcoming adversity. Although I don't know you personally, know that I respect your courage to face your painful thoughts and feelings.

Years ago, Austrian physician and Holocaust survivor, Victor Frankl stated: "Everything can be taken from a man but ... the last of the human freedoms—to choose one's attitude in any given set of circumstances, to choose one's own way."

I want to empower you to respond to *your* loss by making informed, healthy, goal-directed choices. By doing so, you can regain a sense of control, bring hope into your life and ultimately grow through this experience.

3.
A Crisis is in the Eye of the Beholder

How would you define a crisis?

Many people think that a crisis is an overwhelming event. In actuality, a crisis is *our unique experience* in the face of what we perceive to be an overwhelming event. A crisis for me may not be a crisis for you. And, similarly, what you perceive to be a crisis may not be for me.

How we interpret and label our experience will determine whether a particular event leads to feelings of fear, helplessness and even horror—whether our experience rises to the level of a crisis. This process of interpreting and labeling is based on many things like our past, the nature of the event itself and the kind of support we receive after the event—the before, during and after.

Understanding that a crisis is the *human response* to an overwhelming event brings us hope. Although you can't change and undo what's happened in your life (the event), you can choose what you do now and how you interpret and label your experience (your crisis).

4.
What to Do ... Now

What you do during and in the wake of this crisis will depend on what's happened. Have you experienced the loss of a loved one? Are you battling an illness? Have you been injured? Have you been victimized? No matter what's happened, at times you're feeling overwhelmed. This is *your* crisis.

Try to surround yourself with special friends and loved ones. Be there for each other and know that it's okay to feel. Former Prime Minister of Britain Benjamin Disraeli once said, "Never apologize for showing feeling. When you do so, you apologize for truth."

As much as possible, and with the help of people who are close to you, try to obtain facts. Knowing what's happened, or is happening, is generally easier than the unknown. Depending upon the event, it may not be possible to know the facts early on; they may come with time.

While you're vacillating between uncomfortable thoughts and feelings, keep bringing yourself back to your "thinking and problem-solving mode." Take care of your basic needs. Drink lots of fluids, eat small meals, and keep yourself in a safe place.

If at any time you experience difficulty breathing, chest pains or palpitations, or any other disturbing physical reaction, speak with your physician or health care provider immediately. In fact it's a good idea, in general, to make your doctor aware of what you're going through.

The answer to what you need to do now lies within you.

5.
Face Your Feelings

When someone is bleeding profusely, we certainly don't sit back and watch the blood flow. In the same way we shouldn't wait to address the "emotional hemorrhage."

We're quick to deal with people's physical needs—I think of sirens and flashing lights. Yet, we know that those signals are not telling us to move out of the way because someone is *feeling* overwhelmed, painfully alone and scared.

We know that people who take the time to share their feelings, early on, generally fare better down the road. But this doesn't mean that we should force ourselves, or others, to talk. It means that we should have the opportunity to receive the support that *we* need as soon as possible.

For years, I've listened to descriptions of failed family and social relationships, a loss of interest in things once enjoyed, disrupted educational plans, destroyed careers, stress-related illnesses and substance abuse. More often than not, one's pain was linked directly to an overwhelming event. Had emotional needs been attended to early on, during a crisis, perhaps one wouldn't have had to endure years of suffering!

By exposing yourself to your uncomfortable feelings, you can potentially prevent the *acute* difficulties of today from becoming *chronic* problems tomorrow. Let's not wait to address your feelings.

6.
Find the Right People with Whom to Speak

Have you been feeling alone and confused? Are people saying they're "sorry" and embracing you? Are your friends asking you how they can help you? The closeness and support helps, but it's never enough. The pain, emptiness, fear and loneliness continue.

One of the most important things for you to do is to continue to communicate and resist the temptation to shut down, withdraw and avoid others. It's so important to share your thoughts and feelings. The problem with this is that people are not always the best listeners. In fact, those who know you and love you the most are often so disturbed by your situation, themselves, that they may offer impulsive suggestions in an effort to help you to feel better quickly. The reality is that *they* need to feel better quickly!

Your friends and loved ones may tell you that they know what you're going through ... they know how you feel ... that you'll feel better with time ... that it could have been much worse ... that everything will be okay.... These well-intended "band-aid" statements only increase our feelings of aloneness, and lead many people to keep their feelings to themselves.

So, to whom should you turn? And how can you turn off all the advice...?

First, explain to those who care deeply for you that you need to talk. You don't need answers. You need to "vent"—to let out your bottled-up thoughts and feelings.

Many people find comfort in sharing their pain with a friend or loved one who has experienced a similar event. There's a feeling of ... "She understands what I'm going through."

No matter with whom you choose to speak, always remember this: *you are the expert in being you. And no one has the right to tell you how you should feel.*

7.
Turn to Professionals

If there are professionals helping you through this difficult time, share your thoughts and feelings with them. Their knowledge and experience with others who've been through a similar event may help them to understand your situation—and enable them to provide you with sound guidance and support. From doctors and nurses to funeral directors ... emergency responders to attorneys ... these professionals work regularly with people *during* times of crisis.

Consider speaking with a mental health professional, early on—a counselor, social worker, psychologist or psychiatrist. I'm not suggesting that you become engaged in intensive psychotherapy during this crisis. However, these individuals can offer support and a non-judgmental, well-trained empathic ear. Also, consider turning to a member of the clergy—your spiritual leader. So many people cope with and overcome adversity by maintaining a strong spiritual connection.

If you just don't feel comfortable speaking with a professional, consider keeping a journal ... a daily log. By writing your thoughts and feelings about your experience, or even recording them with a small voice recorder, you'll expose yourself to your feelings and jump-start your coping and problem-solving abilities.

8.
How to Help the Children

People frequently ask, "What should I tell the children?" My answer is always, "... the truth." However, information *must* be conveyed at a developmentally appropriate level. For instance, young children don't need to hear every detail of what's happened. That may only confuse and upset them—and likely cause them greater distress.

Tell children what they need to know, don't share more information than they're able to hear or understand, encourage them to articulate their feelings, and answer their questions honestly and directly. And if you don't know the answer, it's okay. Tell them that you don't know.

It's important that you don't lie to children in an effort to protect them—even if the truth is painfully difficult. Children will only come to know the truth sooner or later. And it's generally sooner than later. There's no reason to add additional pain due to feelings of being misled or being lied to. Again, just be careful to share what's appropriate for the child to hear at his or her developmental age. If you're not sure what to share, seek the help of people who work regularly with children such as pediatricians, educators, counselors or child psychologists.

9.
Children Will Learn from This Experience

During a crisis, children, particularly little ones, will take their cues from the adults around them. They'll model the behavior of the adults in their lives. The problem here is that, depending on their age, they may lack the ability to use language to express their thoughts and feelings. Instead, we see reflections of what's going on inside conveyed in their actions outside—their behavior.

Drawing pictures, coloring, or shaping clay can be helpful for children to begin to expose themselves to and to share their feelings with others.

Try as best you can to use your crisis as a powerful learning experience for the children in your life. You're setting the stage for how they'll respond to tragedies, both large and small, for the rest of their lives. Again, for guidance, turn to people who regularly work with children.

Finally, listen to *your* inner voice that will guide you in helping the children in your life.

10.
Peak Emotional Experiences Stay with Us

It's easy for us to recall peak emotional times in our lives. We hold onto memories of births and deaths, celebrations and tragedies. They become imprinted in our minds. They become a part of who we are. They shape our personalities.

If you think about it, when really bad things happen to us, leading to intense emotional reactions, a load of negative stuff gets etched in our minds. What did you take in—a horrible sight, hearing terrible news, physical pain? Whatever it is that you experienced can end up being repetitive sights, sounds, smells—the stuff that can cause you tremendous emotional pain in the future.

But what if we countered painful negative images, words and sensations with healing positive ones?

Whatever you think about, whatever you focus on during a peak emotional experience will stay with you forever! Let the messages in this book be a positive force—healing, proactive information that stays with you and becomes a part of your experience.

11.
Knowledge Is Power

Did you ever notice that when people are sick or injured they become experts on their condition? If they have a lower back injury, they'll tell you all about the lumbar spine. If they have a shoulder problem, they're experts on the rotator cuff. If they're battling cancer, they can tell you about the levels of various proteins in their blood.

We become experts on our physical problems, because knowledge is power. Knowledge gives us the power to act, to ask relevant questions and to make informed decisions. Knowledge gives us back a sense of control that an injury or disease takes away.

In the same way, we can become knowledgeable about our emotional, social, behavioral, physical and spiritual responses during a crisis. I sometimes refer to these as the "hidden trauma."

I want this book to empower you with practical information to help you to understand what's happening to you now. *Knowledge about your experience will give you back a sense of control that adversity seems to have taken away.*

12.
Know What "Traumatic Stress" Is and What It's Not

When we think of *stress,* we generally associate it with the potential wear and tear on our mind and body as we adjust to daily changes and challenges in our lives. Yet there are both negative and positive attributes to stress. On the negative side, stress can compromise our ability to think clearly, cause us to feel anxious, disrupt our ability to sleep and, ultimately, lead to physical illness. On the positive side, stress can be a powerful force that enables us to get things done and be more productive. Some people describe how they work better *under stress—* when they're feeling pressured.

Some events in our lives can be so overwhelming that we perceive a serious threat to our physical well-being, or the well-being of others. We may experience intense feelings of fear, helplessness and horror. We may feel overwhelmed, unsafe, insecure and vulnerable. This is *traumatic stress*—our feelings, thoughts, actions, and physical and spiritual reactions when we're exposed to, or even witness, events that overwhelm our ability to cope.

People experience traumatic stress when they're exposed to a disaster or catastrophe—a plane crash, terrorist attack, the battlefield, or an earthquake. Yet it doesn't have to be a highly publicized event with a two-inch newspaper headline. People also experience traumatic stress during the *personal disasters* that color their lives: facing an illness or injury, dealing with the tragic loss of a loved one, being physically or sexually violated, experiencing an accident, or living through a divorce.

Like stress, *traumatic* stress can also have a positive side. It can be the force that propels people to cultivate a mission and purpose and, ultimately, the ability to live with a new sense of passion. By understanding what traumatic stress is and by knowing that it's a *normal* response to an *abnormal* event you'll be empowered and in a better position to survive and thrive.

13.
What PTSD Is

As I shared with you in the last message, traumatic stress is a *normal* response to an *abnormal* event. We must not confuse traumatic stress with *Posttraumatic Stress Disorder* (PTSD).

PTSD, along with other psychiatric diagnoses, may apply to people who continue to experience ongoing debilitating symptoms after exposure to a traumatic event. Let me explain just a bit.

During a crisis, your brain is bathed with chemicals that are primarily designed to keep you alive. However, these chemicals can "work overtime" causing you to feel anxious, excessively watchful, panicky, angry and depressed. They can certainly compromise your ability to function into the future. However, this book is not about understanding psychiatric criteria, labels and disorders. It's about the potential to prevent them in the first place!

I believe that we're too quick to label people in an effort to regain a sense of control that adversity seems to have taken away. Unfortunately, these labels can be very destructive, in and of themselves. They can lead to a "self-fulfilling prophesy." If you hear it, you begin to associate everything you do as "due to PTSD, *my* disorder."

We can't avoid experiencing losses, illness and other tragedies during our lifetimes. They're part of the human experience. And we certainly can't inoculate ourselves from experiencing traumatic stress. Again, it's a normal response to an abnormal event. However, by having an understanding of what's happening to us, *while it's happening*, and by knowing that our reactions are normal, we can become empowered to work toward regaining a sense of control of our lives.

We can potentially prevent accute stress reactions from becoming chronic and debilitating stress disorders.

14.
Your Past Will Influence Today

When we face a crisis, we deal not only with the event that precipitated it, but our prior experiences as well. Challenging life events unearth our most painful thoughts and feelings. They scratch the emotional scars of our past.

Is this happening to you now? Does it feel like you're "linking with" your past hurt and pain? Know that this reaction is very common and very normal.

What's happened in your past can seem like a double-edged sword. On the one hand, it may provide you with a frame of reference and help you to know that you've made it through a painful time, and that you'll make it through today. On the other hand, your past may have emotionally scarred you, leaving you particularly vulnerable to further hurt. *Traumatic events have a cumulative effect.*

One of the reasons why the terrorist attacks on September 11, 2001 were so difficult for us is that we didn't have a frame of reference. Nearly all of us couldn't draw upon a similar past experience to help us to understand and cope with what we were facing. The events were so different from anything we had experienced before. In essence, we were writing a new book about the kinds of tragedies that impact our lives. We became a nation in crisis!

Awareness and recognition that you're not only experiencing thoughts and feelings about your current crisis, but your past experiences as well, can empower you today, if you *choose* to let them.

15.
An Illness or Injury Can Make It Even More Difficult

Are you sick? Have you been physically harmed? Are you experiencing ongoing pain or discomfort? Are you dealing with changes with your body?

It's important to understand that there's a very real connection between your mind and body. What happens to you physically will impact you emotionally. And your emotions can certainly impact your physical well-being too.

If you're experiencing physical pain and discomfort, discuss this with your doctor. Pain is your body's natural mechanism that signals to you that something is wrong. Similarly, if you're experiencing ongoing *emotional pain* such as feelings of intense anxiety, feelings of panic or depression, or ongoing sleeplessness due to racing thoughts or disturbing dreams, discuss this with a health professional as well. Medication and other strategies can dramatically help to alleviate your discomfort.

Why is it that physical illness or injury makes it more difficult for us to cope?

Physical changes, pain and scarring are cues that can rekindle painful thoughts and feelings. Simply put, it's hard to escape what's happened!

A physical illness or injury may also necessitate ongoing medical care. Do you need to stay in a hospital? Are you visiting doctors regularly? Are you undergoing physical therapy? Do you feel like a "professional patient?"

I'm thinking of the aloneness that you're likely experiencing right now. And I feel so privileged that you're reading this.

There are many strategies that can ease physical pain and discomfort, such as relaxation techniques, cognitive (thinking) coping skills, nutritional support, behavioral techniques and medication. I'll discuss some of these in this book. Mental health service providers and other healthcare professionals can empower you with more strategies.

Once again, if you're struggling with ongoing physical or emotional pain or discomfort, speak with your doctor. Don't wait and suffer in silence!

16.
Beware of the Impact of Your Crisis on Others

Several years ago, I received a call from a television news program. I was asked to comment on a story about a girl who grew up with her father, a Vietnam veteran. Throughout her childhood and early adulthood, she experienced daily doses of stories: her father's painful recollections, his need to avoid certain places, and his feelings of jumpiness with every loud noise. After her father died, this young woman began to experience the very same symptoms that her father did, even though she was never directly exposed to Vietnam.

I'm sharing this story with you because it demonstrates what I call the *vicarious power* of traumatic events—the "emotional fall-out" people face when a loved one lives through a crisis.

As you struggle today, there will likely be others who are impacted by your experience, maybe your father, mother, brother, sister, friend, teacher, colleague, nurse or doctor. While it's not your responsibility to care for them, allow yourself to understand *their* feelings of anxiety, frustration, anger, guilt or fear. By doing so, you'll appreciate where some of their comments, suggestions and advice are coming from.

When I speak with clients, I frequently caution them to "beware of the hidden victims" such as family members, friends and others who may have been indirectly hurt.

Once again, becoming knowledgeable about what's happening to you, and those around you, will enable you to regain a sense of control.

17.
The Myth of Clear-Cut Stages

There's no "standard way" in which people respond to an overwhelming life experience. Some of us respond immediately, while others may experience a delayed reaction, sometimes months or even years down the road. Some people's reactions may last for a long period of time. For others, traumatic stress reactions are short-lived. The intensity of our reactions will vary as well.

What stages do people go through during a crisis? Often, there is little structure when dealing with people's reactions. Our response to an overwhelming event will be colored by many factors like genetics, our physical condition, our past experience, and the kind of support we receive today.

While people seem to experience similar reactions during a crisis like shock, denial, anger and depression, the timeframe and order in which we experience these reactions varies from person to person.

Rather than trying to fit yourself into some pre-determined stage of coping or healing, recognize that *no one is more of an expert on your emotional needs than you. No one has the right to question your beliefs or to tell you how you should respond to your crisis!*

By reading the messages in this book, and by gaining a deeper understanding of what's happening to you when things are not okay, you'll move through your own stages of healing.

18.
Your Feelings ...
Your Unique Perceptions

It's difficult to describe what a feeling is—the deepest meaning that we attribute to our experience. I often say that feelings are the stuff that's hardest to talk about—our most personal experience.

It's important to understand that your feelings don't just exist, but that they're caused by the meanings and beliefs that you attach to your experiences. The reason we *feel* good when we receive a gift is not because it's gold and shiny, but because of the beliefs that we attach to that shiny thing. These beliefs stem from associations that we've made from our past experiences.

In the same way, when a tragedy strikes, all the negative, scary, sad feelings we experienced during past tragic situations will color the way we feel about this new event—but we may not consciously be aware that this is happening. As an analogy, if you scratch a pair of eyeglasses, what you see through those glasses will be affected by the size and depth of the scratch. However, you generally won't consciously link that scratch and the blurriness it creates to the exact day that you dropped your glasses on the ground.

Because of the uniqueness of your history, you're entitled to your unique feelings. And no one has the right to tell you how you should feel.

Treasure the uniqueness of you!

19.
What You're Feeling ... Now

I want the messages in this book to ease your emotional pain, keep you functioning and lessen the likelihood of ongoing suffering. As I've said, a critical step in doing so is to begin to acknowledge and face your feelings. Let me help you to understand what you might be feeling now.

Early on, during a crisis, it's very common for us to experience emotional shock. You may feel extremely anxious, nervous, fearful and sometimes even panicky. Or, you may feel nothing but numbness. Just like the physical state of shock, emotional shock keeps us alive and protects us from further harm.

Denial is also a normal reaction, particularly early on. You may not feel or experience the full impact of what's happened. Denial is a mechanism that prevents you from feeling too much too quickly.

You may also experience dissociation, where things don't seem real, they seem spacey. A woman recently turned to me at a wake and said that it felt "surreal." Some people describe feeling as if they're watching themselves in a movie. You may emotionally disconnect yourself from anyone, and sometimes anything, associated with your experience. Have you been feeling numb?

Some of us experience flashbacks, where every detail of what's happened is vividly played back over and over again. We may keep feeling, hearing, smelling, tasting, and seeing what's happened.

Other common emotional reactions are feelings of aloneness, emptiness, sadness, disbelief, resentment, helplessness, hopelessness, grief, anger and guilt. Guilt is one of the most difficult emotions for us to deal with. You may feel in some way responsible for what's happened. And you may find yourself frequently saying, "If only...."

Are you *linking with* (connecting emotionally with) this message? Please stay with me. By knowing that your feelings are very common and very normal, and by exposing yourself to them, you'll continue on your journey toward healing.

Remember to share your feelings with others and know that, indeed, *it's okay not to be okay* during this challenging time in your life.

20.
Not Wanting to Live

Living through a crisis can feel overwhelming. And it's not uncommon for us to want to avoid or escape our painful reality.

Thoughts of never waking up or even ending your life may feel like a solution, particularly when you're emotionally and physically weakened and vulnerable. It may seem like a way to stop all the hurt. However, it's critically important to understand that taking this action results in the most permanent consequence—a life-ending consequence for you, and incredibly severe life-altering consequences for those who care for you and need you in their lives.

If you're having frequent thoughts of harming yourself or others, please reach out to someone, such as a doctor, counselor, spiritual leader, relative or a special friend. So many people have told me that at some point they had these thoughts. I can't tell you how many people in the months and years after their experience were beyond thankful that they didn't act on them!

I'm not going to tell you that time heals all wounds, because it doesn't. What time does do is give us the opportunity to work through the normal phases of grieving and learn to survive. It's been said, many times, that there's no way around grieving, only through it. What you're feeling now is normal—uncomfortable and extremely painful—but normal.

21.
Turn Off the Feeling Switch and Change What You're Doing

In an early message, I discussed the importance of finding the *right people* with whom to speak about your feelings. And as I've said over and over again, exposing ourselves early on to uncomfortable and painful feelings can help us on the journey of healing.

However, facing your feelings, particularly *during* a crisis, is easier said than done. Having some practical strategies will make it easier.

If I could convey one message to everyone who was living through a crisis, it would be this: *instead of trying to change the way you feel, change what you're doing*. Focus on your actions rather than your emotions. Although we have little control of our feelings, we often have control of the choices we make concerning what we do. I recognize that if you're sick, injured or immobilized in a hospital bed, this can be difficult, if not impossible.

By changing what you're doing, physically, your feelings will change. Your brain will respond to physical movement and activity with the release of neurotransmitters. These chemicals will naturally adjust your feelings. Also, by changing what you do, you shift from left-brain language processing (labeling your experience), to right-brain functioning. You'll give your thinking and feeling some time-off.

During painful times in our lives, it's easy and very common for us become consumed with our feelings. If you find yourself unable to stop "taking your emotional pulse," and unable to stop over-analyzing your feelings, turn off the "feeling switch" by changing what you're doing.

22.
Professionals Can Empower You to Help Yourself

I've had the privilege of counseling with people for over twenty years. And during this time, I've come to know that those who seek professional help *already* have a desire to make things better in their lives. If they didn't, they wouldn't be in my office in the first place.

It's not a sign of weakness to speak with a professional counselor or therapist. It's a sign of strength! As I've said previously, it takes courage to face our uncomfortable feelings.

Obtain a referral from a close friend or loved one. Or turn to your healthcare provider or spiritual leader. Beyond being certified or licensed, knowledgeable and experienced, the single most important variable in finding a professional counselor or therapist is that you feel comfortable with the person with whom you speak.

It's also important to know that there's no single type of counseling or therapy, or any specific technique that will help all people all of the time, to deal with all kinds of problems.

If you're more comfortable with the idea of attending a support group than working one-on-one with a counselor or therapist, there are countless organizations (churches, synagogues, community centers, health organizations, hospitals, clinics, school support personnel) that will be able to guide you to a group in your area. Local publications and the Internet can also provide information about organizations that offer support groups.

One last thought. When someone is in trouble in the water, struggling to swim, we may throw him a life preserver. That's certainly not the time to begin swimming lessons! In the same way, when someone is in the midst of a crisis, that's not the time to begin intensive psychotherapy. A good counselor or therapist will provide *support* and help you to utilize *your* resources, your "emotional life preservers," to empower you to help yourself.

23.
Your Thoughts ...
Your Perspectives and
Beliefs

Are you having difficulty focusing? Is your mind wandering? Are you finding yourself playing back the tape of what's happened?

During a crisis, it's difficult for us to concentrate. Overwhelming events interfere with our thinking and negatively impact our ability to make sound decisions and choices. It's for this reason that the messages in this book are concise. It's also the reason I repeat key concepts over and over again. I'm sure you've noticed! Please, take your time to absorb this information. This book is not designed to be a "quick read."

Early on, when we face a traumatic event, the right half of our brain is engaged in "fight-or-flight" mode, working to keep us physically alive. Shortly thereafter, the left side, the verbal "thinking" part of our brain, kicks-in and we begin to process and label what's happening. At this time our attention span is shorter than usual, it's difficult to make even simple decisions and we're highly suggestible and vulnerable. With that "tape" of the event playing over and over, our minds are in a state of confusion. Does this sound familiar to you?

Painful experiences will color your thoughts. They'll influence the way you perceive situations and impact your beliefs. Therefore, *now is not the time to make major decisions in your life* such as moving, leaving your partner or quitting your job. In fact, I often suggest that we never make important decisions during peak emotional experiences. Hence the old saying, "Sleep on it." However, if your circumstance requires that you do so, turn to those in your life who assure you, "I'm here for you," or those who ask, "What can I do for you?"

Beyond knowing what's happening to your thinking abilities, you'll benefit from some very practical cognitive (thought) strategies that can guide you through your crisis. Stay with me.

24.
Tackle Your Thoughts

What we focus on, what we think about, becomes our experience. This is why it's normal for us to feel so horrible when bad things happen. We have beliefs—our thoughts about what's happened, and as we focus on and think about them, we feel the pain and hurt.

Although we can't turn back time and undo what's happened in your life, you can become aware of, take control and tackle your thinking. *You can choose your focus.*

If twelve people were exposed to the same event that you're experiencing, some of their reactions would be the same as yours, and some would be very different. It depends upon each individual's beliefs—their thoughts about the event and the specific aspects of the event on which they choose to focus.

So, what can you do now? How do you go about changing what you focus on, what you think about?

When your home gets too hot or too cold, what do you do? You put on a sweater or sweatshirt, or you check the thermostat and make an adjustment. In the same way, when you find yourself experiencing a strong, uncomfortable feeling, check your "emotional thermostat" to see what you're focusing on, what you're thinking about. Then, make an adjustment in what you're saying to yourself. *Use your feelings as signals to pay closer attention to your thoughts, and their impact on your feelings and actions.*

Let me give you an example. You notice that you're feeling very nervous and irritable. Ask yourself, "What am I focusing on? What am I thinking about?" "I'm thinking ... if only I had...." Then, make an adjustment in what you're saying to yourself— "It's really not helpful for me to start the 'if only game.' I need to get myself up for a walk!"

At first, this concept of "adjusting your thinking" may sound simplistic. You'll need to practice. However, as you read through this book, you'll see that your thoughts will dramatically impact how you feel.

25.
Focus on the Facts

A powerful way to take control of your thoughts and give your feelings a break is by focusing on the facts. What exactly happened? When? Who was there? What did it sound like? What was I told?

As you think about the facts, consciously slow down your mental tape of the images so that you can focus on what you know has happened or is happening. As I've indicated before, your experience has led you to feel a loss of control. By slowing down the tape and focusing on what you *do know*, you'll regain a sense of control.

If you don't know the facts, work to obtain them. Here's where a close friend or loved one can help. Also, speak with professionals who are involved. Take notes. This information may help you down the road, particularly if you become involved with the legal system. Depending upon what's happened, you may also wish to speak with an attorney. Sound legal guidance can empower you.

While you focus on the facts, be careful not to become consumed with them. While knowledge will help to give back a sense of control, ruminating and rehashing every detail of what's happened will not only be painful, but exhausting! If you catch yourself doing this, talk to yourself. Say "This isn't helpful for me. I need to focus on what I can do now." If the facts become too painful to handle, share your feelings with others and again, change what you're doing.

26.
Stop the Mental Snowball

When you were a child, did you build a snowman? Do you remember pushing a small, lumpy ball of snow around on the ground until it started to grow? Eventually it got so big that you couldn't budge it. It became the bottom of your snowman.

This same concept can be applied to our thinking. We start off with a thought and then roll it around in our mind. As it gets bigger, as we build on our thinking, it becomes harder to handle and maneuver. Becoming aware that you're doing this is very helpful in maintaining control of your thoughts and helping yourself to feel better.

The next time you find yourself feeling overwhelmed, picture your mental snowball growing as your thinking begins spiraling. Learn to catch yourself *early on* and say to yourself that you'll, "stop here, before this boulder becomes any bigger." *You have the ability to control what you're thinking and to adjust how you feel.*

27.
About Your Actions

Although there are common reactions during a crisis, each of our specific reactions is as different as our unique personalities. Some of us withdraw, "space-out" and become non-communicative. Others do the exact opposite, acting impulsively, walking and pacing with seemingly boundless energy. Still others avoid thoughts, feelings, conversations, activities, people, and places associated with the event.

How have you been responding? Are you shutting down? Are you withdrawing? Are you overly outgoing? Or, are you avoiding all things associated with what's happened?

It's particularly important for you to know that *how you respond, how you choose to act during this crisis will become part of who you are forever. Not only that, but how others act will become a part of your perceptions as well.*

While we can't always control the events in our lives, we can control our thoughts—and how we respond to them—by what we choose to do. We can make decisions to regain control at a time when it feels like we've lost control. You've already made the decision to read this book, so you're taking control right now.

28.
What to Do ... Now

What you do now will depend upon what's happened. Are you spending time in a hospital, visiting doctors' offices, speaking with police detectives, consulting with an attorney or attending the funeral of a loved one?

If you're feeling that you're not safe right now, share this with someone in your life. And don't hesitate to turn to the authorities for immediate help.

Whenever it's possible, try to stick with or return to your usual routine. We're all creatures of habit and our daily routines provide us with familiarity and a sense of control. Resist the urge to avoid people or to stay inside your home. Keeping yourself physically isolated from the world around you for too long can compromise your ability to heal.

If you find yourself avoiding certain situations such as leaving your home or driving a car, try to face your discomfort directly and work through it, perhaps with the help of a friend. Once we start avoiding things, avoidance can become a problem in and of itself. For example, by not driving a car after an accident, it may become too easy to avoid driving in the future.

Sometimes it's easier if the task is approached gradually. In the same way that we encourage a child who falls off his bike to get back on, it's important for us to keep getting "back on that bike" in the aftermath of a traumatic event. If you find yourself regularly avoiding situations, consider speaking with a mental health professional.

29.
Limit Communication

When you first read the title of this message you may wonder why, after all my discussion of the need to share your thoughts and feelings with others, I would suggest that you *limit* communication. Stay with me.

With rapidly growing technology, we're able to communicate better today than at any time before. And while there are no doubt many benefits from improved communication, there are also potential dangers. For example, how many of us will forever have the image of a plane crashing into the World Trade Center imprinted in our minds? It was nearly impossible to escape the daily doses of televised video clips.

During a crisis you're highly suggestible and vulnerable. If there's mass communication, media attention being drawn to your experience, limit your exposure. People face very real traumatic stress reactions by watching disturbing events on television. Similarly, be careful not to become consumed with newspaper and Internet stories about the event. While *some* information may provide you with answers, too much information or factually incorrect information may only serve to overwhelm and frustrate you.

And what about cell phones, email and text messaging? While we're fortunate to live in a time of growing communication, this rapid technological advance can also overwhelm us. You can easily experience "information overload." Is this happening to you? If so, set limits. For example, keep your cell phone out of your bedroom. As the title of this message says, limit communication.

30.
Understand "Secondary Victimization"

Depending on what's happened, it's sometimes necessary to speak with the police, firefighters, paramedics, nurses, doctors, attorneys or other professionals so they may investigate and gather information. While you're overwhelmed by your emotions, they require only the facts. And sometimes these folks are not as understanding, compassionate and empathic as we need them to be. Some people become "secondarily victimized" by a "fact hungry" system, including the media, that they perceive to be insensitive. Is this happening in your life?

If you're finding yourself feeling angry with those who are investigating and trying to understand your experience, recognize that this reaction is very common. While those who are firing questions at you may neither be the cause of what's happened, nor have anything at all to do with it, they can become scapegoats for your displaced feelings of frustration.

Many people suffer from being secondarily victimized by our legal process. Having worked hard at regaining control of your post-trauma life, you may be called into court to testify about the event months or even years after it happened. This experience may very well throw you into emotional turmoil all over again.

If you're currently in the situation where you have to repeat your story, or if it's likely that you'll have to do this in the future, know that it's very common and very normal to feel emotional pain again. Remember, what you focus on will become your experience. Your thinking will directly influence how you feel. Hold onto this book and revisit these messages.

31.
The Pain of Anniversaries

Anniversaries not only mark a significant period in our lives, but also prompt us to review where we've been and where we're going. They're powerful cues that rekindle your thoughts and feelings.

The anniversary of this crisis, as well as other traumatic events you've experienced, may cause an "anniversary effect." You'll likely experience painful feelings down the road. This is entirely normal. But now you'll be empowered with knowledge, and have specific coping strategies you've learned from this book.

Take action and use these strategies again so the intensity and duration of your reaction will be more manageable than you originally experienced.

32.
About Your Physical Reactions

Although there are many kinds of traumatic experiences that can affect us, there aren't nearly as many kinds of physical reactions. In fact, we respond the same way to a car backfiring as we do to a gunshot, with the fight-or-flight response. It's not until we begin thinking about our experience that we become aware of and begin to understand what's happening.

During your crisis, your body will work overtime to regain physical balance and well-being. It's common to experience muscle aches and physical weakness.

You may have headaches, backaches and stomachaches. And, you may find yourself using the bathroom constantly. If you notice blood in your urine or stools, please contact your doctor.

It's also very common to experience changes in your sleep patterns and to have disturbing dreams. In fact, sleep problems are among the most common reactions we face. Has this been the case with you? I often say that our mind is working overtime to try to make sense of the senseless.

If at any time you're having difficulty breathing, or experiencing chest pains or palpitations, you should be seen by a doctor to make sure it's not a medical problem requiring immediate attention.

Has your appetite changed? Is it difficult to even think about food? This is not uncommon during a crisis. Even if you have little appetite, I encourage you to drink and eat a little at a time. Dehydration and a lack of good nutrition has a very real negative effect on your healing process—making you feel much worse physically and further weakening your emotional well-being.

33.
Limit or Avoid Alcohol and Caffeine

During times of crisis, some of us consume beverages containing alcohol and caffeine. Historically, people have turned to the calming effects of alcohol to numb the hurt and to the stimulating effects of caffeine to energize them. Is this true for you?

During this time of intense emotion, the seemingly beneficial effects of alcohol and caffeine can be misleading. Alcohol is a depressant that may intensify your negative experience, and caffeine is a stimulant that may increase your feelings of anxiety and agitation, and interfere with your ability to sleep.

Though it's important to drink plenty of fluids, avoid drinking large quantities of caffeinated beverages like coffee and colas. And although a glass of red wine or a beer may help to quell your nerves, be careful not to become reliant on it to "self-medicate" your hurt.

34.
Excessively Watchful and Jumpy

Have you become excessively, and sometimes obsessively, watchful and cautious? In all likelihood, you're not paranoid or "losing it!" You're experiencing a basic survival mechanism called *hypervigilance*. It has historically protected us, by keeping us on high alert after traumatic exposure.

Although you may no longer be in danger, you may continue to experience intense feelings of nervousness and watchfulness. If this happens to you, consciously label it—"There's the hypervigilance again." And assure yourself that the danger has passed—"I'm handling this now."

Once again, you have the ability to regain a feeling of control by adjusting your thinking.

It's also very common to experience an increased or exaggerated startle response, making you jumpy when there's a loud noise or when someone walks up behind you. This is a very common and very normal reaction for someone who's living through a crisis, particularly if he/she has been involved in an event where there were loud noises and lots of stimulation.

This startle response usually becomes less problematic over time. If you continue to be disturbed by *any* physical problems, speak with your healthcare provider.

35.
Meds or No Meds

You may be encouraged by a family member or a friend to take medication—making you wonder whether it could be the solution to your emotional turmoil and pain. Or, you may simply wonder whether medication may help you to get through this difficult time. The best person with whom to speak is your physician, who knows you and your medical history. But in order for your doctor to be able to prescribe the right course of action, you must be forthcoming about what has occurred and the *specific* problems you're having.

There isn't a magic pill that will cure a traumatic stress reaction—a normal response to an abnormal event. What proper medication can do is help to address some of the *symptoms* that are adversely impacting your ability to function and getting in the way of your emotional healing.

If you're physically exhausted from lack of sleep, if your headaches inhibit clear thought, if your mind is racing with disconnected thoughts, or if you're experiencing frequent feelings of panic, then you will not be able to focus on the issues and strategies that can help you emotionally.

While you may have the ability within yourself to manage this crisis, medication can be very helpful when symptoms continue to interfere with and compromise your ability to cope and function.

36.
"Mind-Body
Disconnection"

You've probably heard of the "mind-body connection." It refers to how our emotional selves interact with our physical selves. In other words, your mind can affect how your body functions. And your body can affect how your mind works—what you're thinking and feeling.

If you're sick or if you've been physically harmed, you now have constant cues from your illness or injury reminding you that you're *not okay.*

There's a strategy that can help you. I refer to it as, "Mind-Body Disconnection." *Instead of focusing on the interaction, the connectedness between your mind and body, try separating the two.* You can say to yourself, "I am not my body. My body is the system within which I live my life. While my body may be sick/hurt, my mind is strong!" You may want to include, "My soul rests within my body. My body is the temple for my soul."

I'm not trying to open the door to a deep spiritual or philosophical discussion here. Instead, I want you to understand the enormous potential of your thinking—the process occurring within your mind, not your body. By doing so, you'll have another coping strategy that will enable you to overcome and consciously separate your *self* from physical discomfort and pain.

37.
The Power of Breathing

During a crisis, it's not uncommon for your breathing to change, in order to help you to manage the stress of your experience. At times, your breathing may become rapid, bringing oxygen into your system to enable you to respond quickly to further danger. But this very same rapid breathing may also cause you to feel anxious, panicky and very uncomfortable.

So, what can you do? Let me share a great technique that will help you take control of your breathing so that it once again becomes a positive, rather than a negative, to your physical and emotional well-being.

First, take the phone off the hook and turn off the ringer on your cell phone. Sit, or lie down, and make yourself comfortable. Close your eyes and become aware of your breathing. For the moment, don't try to change it, just become aware of, and focus on, your breathing. Some thoughts may come into your mind and if they do, just chase them away, continuing to concentrate only on your breathing. Notice each time you inhale and each time you exhale. With each exhalation, think the word, "relax."

Next, take a slow deep breath through your nose, hold it for a few seconds and then slowly exhale through your mouth. Do this several times. You'll find yourself becoming more relaxed with each breath you take.

There's a reason why people, from athletes to soon-to-be-moms, are encouraged to become aware of their breathing and to build a repertoire of breathing techniques. Learning to control your breathing can become a powerful physical and emotional force that will enable you to cope more effectively with adversity.

38.
Exercise

In an early message, I described how you could turn off the "feeling switch" by changing what you're doing. Again, physical activity can have a profound effect on what you think and how you feel. If you're able to exercise, it can be very helpful. It can enable you to expend some of the energy that's built-up inside you. Exercise can also release neurotransmitters—chemicals in your brain that will help you feel better.

If you had exercised regularly before this crisis, try to keep exercising now, even if it's only an abbreviated part of your regular routine. If you weren't exercising before, I urge you to find something to do now, to give yourself a *physical release* for the emotional energy that's built up inside you. If you're able, take the time to go out for a walk. Again, what you do with your body will affect how you're thinking and how you're feeling.

39.
Conquering Your Sleep Difficulties

As I said previously, nearly everyone who faces a crisis experiences sleep difficulties. It's probably the single most common symptom we face. And if it's not difficult to get to sleep or stay asleep, it's having those disturbing dreams.

So, what can you do?

First, find a safe and quiet place to sleep. If possible, leave your cell phone out of the bedroom and turn off the ringer on your home phone. Be sure not to have caffeinated beverages in the evening. Try listening to soft music. Have a warm glass of milk. Take a warm bath. Try reading or writing. Use your bed only for sleeping and intimacy. And try the breathing technique.

If you just can't sleep or if any other physical reactions continue to be a problem for you, speak with your doctor. There are medications that can help you to sleep. Also, consider speaking with a mental health professional. There are number of helpful strategies including deep muscle relaxation, visual imagery techniques, meditation, hypnosis, relaxation and stress management techniques that can be very helpful.

40.
Turn to Spirituality

Many people have strong spiritual responses during and in the wake of a crisis. Some are very angry and withdraw from worship. They question their religious beliefs and feel a sense of betrayal by wondering why their experience is happening and why they weren't protected from harm. Others have the opposite reaction, uncharacteristically turning to frequent prayer.

Are you suffering from a crisis of faith? Or are you feeling an unusually strong connection to it? These are both normal reactions. Take some time to sort through your thoughts and feelings. Spirituality and faith have a way of finding their way back into your heart, where you can choose how to celebrate or relax your beliefs. If you remain in crisis, the best person with whom to speak is your spiritual leader. While medical doctors have the knowledge and skills to help heal the body, clergy have the knowledge and skills to help heal the spirit.

I've found that when we're faced with the most overwhelming experiences in our lives, spirituality and faith can provide us with answers to our *most* difficult and profound questions. They can offer us hope at a time when we need it.

41.
Beyond Resiliency

We hear about the "resilient child." And we're told that we should strive to be more resilient.

What does it mean to be resilient anyway?

Resiliency is often defined as the ability to bounce or spring back—and return to its original form.

I don't believe that resiliency should be *our goal.* I don't believe that bouncing or springing back after one of the most challenging times in your life is possible. A crisis changes us and creates a "new normal."

Let's not settle for being the way we were if there's a possibility for us to grow from an experience!

I encourage you to look beyond resiliency. The messages that follow will offer you hope by empowering you to see the enormous potential that a crisis can bring.

42.
Crisis and Opportunity

During and in the wake of a crisis, some people seem to "get stuck." They withdraw, shut down and become reclusive—staying inside, closing off the world around them. They begin a pattern of avoiding people, places and things. Do you see yourself as getting stuck?

Other people use the painful energy from their crisis to make *destructive* choices. They turn to alcohol and drugs, or become engaged in serious conflicts with their families, friends and coworkers.

I have a passion for working with people *during times of crisis* because I believe that the pool of painful energy inside you presents enormous potential. It can provide the fuel that propels you to make *constructive* choices. It can open the door to opportunity!

If your emotional and physical wounds are still raw, it may be too soon to see this potential now. But there will come a time when you begin looking ahead. Stay with me, or come back when you're ready, and begin to see the opportunities that a crisis can bring.

43.
Cultivate a Mission and a New Sense of Purpose

Years ago, I spoke with a shy, teenage girl in the hospital. She experienced a tragedy that was all over the news. While focusing on her story, and on the feelings churning beneath her words, I said softly, "There's a mission here for you. There's a purpose in all of this." She recoiled, glared into my eyes and said, "Nothing good could come out of this."

For several years, indeed nothing positive seemed to come from her horrible experience. I watched as she lived through a highly publicized legal case. And I questioned the appropriateness of what I had said. I thought that I had projected my need for her to get better. Why would I say something about a mission or purpose to someone who was facing the worst experience in her life?

I share this story with you because this seemingly shy girl ultimately cultivated a mission and purpose. She harnessed the energy from her experience, the intense anger and pain, and used it to propel herself to achieve. Today she's very well known and respected, and does so much to help others—*because of her tragedy.* She reinforced my belief of the potential that a crisis can bring, even if we can't see that potential for a while.

Right now, it may be hard to find meaning for what's happened in your life. And it may simply be too soon for you to choose this road. But I hope that you too will ultimately come to see that through adversity you can cultivate a mission and a new sense of purpose in your life.

44.
From Victim to Survivor and Ultimately ... Thriver

A ***victim*** is someone who's been harmed and who's suffering.

A ***survivor*** is someone who, despite hardship and adversity, continues to function.

A ***thriver*** is someone who grows and flourishes.

You can move from being a victim to a survivor and ultimately, a thriver. While it's certainly okay not to be okay during a crisis, you have the capacity to ultimately grow and flourish from your experience. You can be better than okay!

Instead of seeing yourself as a wilting rose, begin to see yourself as a badly bruised bud that still has the potential for a beautiful and lasting bloom.

45.
A Time to Grow

Did you ever notice that when things are going smoothly in your life, when you're comfortable, you tend to go with the flow and time seems to fly by?

And when *bad* things happen, when adversity rears its ugly head, everything seems to move in slow motion. You're thinking all the time. Your mind is filled with overwhelming, confusing and painful thoughts about what's happened.

If you drive with your eyes focused on the rearview mirror, you'll see only where you've been. You may even crash. However, if you focus on the road ahead, you'll see where you're going. Your destination!

In the same way, if you focus on adversity, the painful experiences in your life, you'll feel only the hurt, pain, and sorrow of that time. However, if you challenge yourself to look ahead and identify a destination, a goal, a purpose, then you'll have the opportunity to grow.

Now, don't get me wrong. I'm not saying that in the immediate wake of a tragedy we should sit down, while sobbing, and ask ourselves, "How can I grow from this?" Certainly, no one would choose to experience a tragedy as a way to make a life change. But when a crisis presents itself, we have an opportunity to grow.

Look around you. People who've achieved the most in life haven't always had the easiest lives. A crisis often provides the unique fuel that drives so many people to achieve.

*Your experience, this crisis, presents an opportunity—
an opportunity that can propel you to set goals, make
decisions and take action!*

46.
Reflect on Others Who've Grown

Take a few moments to consider some exemplary people who indeed grew *because of adversity.* You may recognize these stories.

A young girl born to unwed teenage parents grew up in poverty. As a child, she was molested and raped. Today, she's one of the most influential people in the world, not only living her dream, but through her popular talk show and other meaningful ventures, giving so many others opportunities to live theirs. She frequently tells her story and bears her emotional scars as a way to inspire and encourage others to begin their emotional healing. She uses the adversity that she faced, turning it into opportunity for herself and millions of others.

One girl was seriously injured and another girl was killed, both at the hands of drunk drivers. Their mothers then joined forces to develop Mothers Against Drunk Driving. Today, MADD is the largest crime victims' assistance organization in the world.

A six-year-old boy was abducted and murdered. His father then worked to become an advocate for victims' rights and missing children. With his wife, he co-founded the National Center for Missing & Exploited Children. His passion for justice led to the development of the popular crime-fighting television program, America's Most Wanted.

A young athlete, a cyclist, developed cancer. He not only beat the disease, but won the Tour de France again and again. He taught the world to *LiveStrong!*

In searching for your mission and purpose, look inside yourself. The answer is there. It may not be as publicly notable as these examples, but it can be just as glorious and life-affirming. And it's there for you to find!

47.
Focus on the Ideal You

What would you be like if you were the "ideal you?" How would you speak to your family and friends? Would you smile and say "hello" to strangers? How would you respond when you made a mistake? What would enable you to feel happy? What kind of work would you do?

Remember that we're highly suggestible and vulnerable during and in the wake of a crisis. And what we think about, what we focus on will become our experience. So consider the potential of focusing on the "ideal you" ... now!

Rather than being consumed with hurt, rehashing your painful thoughts over and over again, *choose to focus your thoughts on the way you would ideally like to be—how you would like to see yourself.* Consider modeling yourself after someone whose qualities you like and admire.

People who perceive themselves as being very *different* from the way they would ideally like to be, are typically anxious, frustrated and in conflict. However, those who feel a sense of congruence, or *likeness* between the way they see themselves and their ideal self, tend to be happier and fulfilled.

Think about this. People who undergo a physical makeover begin with a vision, an idea of how they would like to look. Computer simulation can help them to see their new body. In the same way, begin by envisioning the way you would ideally like to be. And by focusing on this vision, by rehearsing it over and over again in your mind, you'll move in the direction of becoming the ideal you.

One last thought. While it's generally important for us to "enjoy the moment" and to "stay in the now," a crisis compromises our ability to be okay in the present. Having a goal, a destination, a vision of how we would like to be gives us hope and a sense of control.

48.
Set Goals

In order for you to "become" the way you would ideally like to be, how you would like to see yourself, you'll benefit from having a practical formula. So, here it is. In the remaining messages of this book, I'm going to help you to harness the energy from your crisis and use it to:

1. Set realistic goals
2. Make decisions, and
3. Take action.

There are many great books and programs that deal with goal-setting. I'm going to address the topic from a unique perspective, from the vantage point of you. You're seizing a critical opportunity. You're utilizing the energy *from your crisis* to propel you to achieve your goals.

There are three basic steps to follow:

1. Record your goals. Every goal-setting program that I know has a consistent element. They place great importance on writing goals down. People who commit their goals to writing are simply more likely to achieve them.

Be sure that the goals that you set are realistic and attainable. Goals will help you to identify your mission, your purpose and your destination.

2. Establish a time line. Identify short-term (days), middle-term (weeks) and long-term goals (years). Also, establish specific categories like personal goals, family goals, education goals and work goals. Seeing your goals on paper will help you to identify a need for change.

3. Plan to achieve your goals incrementally. Plan on taking small steps, increasing gradually as your comfort level increases. For example, if you establish a short-term goal to be around people more, try being with one person for a set time, then more than one for a little longer.

Once again, if your feelings are still raw, this process may be premature for you. But I encourage you to give it a try as soon as you can. Whether you choose to work on being more assertive, to write a book about your experience, to plant a garden, to start a foundation to increase awareness of a problem that has impacted your life, establishing goals will help you to re-focus your thoughts on *your destination*—where you would like to see yourself.

If you tap into the pool of energy that your crisis has created within you, there's truly no limit to your potential.

49.
Make Decisions and Take Action

So much of what happens in our lives results from our decisions. This is often why it's so difficult for us when we face a tragedy. We naturally see what's happened as the result of our decisions. We blame ourselves and we feel guilty. If we don't perceive what's happened as the result of our decisions, we often believe that the tragedy was the result of someone else's decisions/actions.

Whether we're feeling guilty about causing the event or feeling anger towards those we feel were in some way responsible, the reality of our loss still exists.

Remember, whatever you decide to focus on, whatever you choose to think about, will become your experience. *And what you think and do during this crisis, during this peak emotional time in your life, will stay with you forever.*

Although establishing goals and making decisions are a constructive way to use your energy, unless you *take action* to reach them, goals are no different than a colorful map that never gets used.

When is it best to act on your decisions and to work toward achieving your goals?

There's no simple answer. There's no rulebook or time line for your crisis. Some people will act immediately or soon after a tragedy. Others will wait to act, taking some time to heal.

Regardless of your timing, when you choose to make a decision and take action, you'll be consciously making a choice and, therefore, you'll be taking control of your life.

50.
Rehearse the Attainment of Your Goals

During this crisis, you've been consumed with your thoughts and feelings. And if you've been focusing only on what's happened, in a sense, you've been rehearsing for a painful life experience.

Instead, let's rehearse the attainment of your goals, your dreams, your aspirations. *Let's refocus and redirect the enormous energy inside you and use it to catapult you to achieve them.* Think of your goals over and over again. Create little movies in your mind where you see and hear yourself as the ideal you achieving your goals. Ultimately, begin to replace your rehearsed "movies" with real actions.

Once you've rehearsed the attainment of your goals, made decisions and taken action, keep taking action until you get the results that you want. It may take a while and you may need to adjust your approach. People who achieve know that it takes time.

Establishing realistic goals that reflect the way you would ideally like to be, rehearsing them in your mind, making thoughtful decisions, and taking action, is a unique path that will empower you to live through and overcome adversity.

While it's okay not to be okay during your crisis, indeed, you have the capacity to be better than okay! Thank you for the privilege of letting me be here for you during this difficult, yet opportune time in your life.

Appendix A

A Personal Message
for All Caregivers

Firefighters race into buildings, into the smoke and flames, ultimately to save lives. In the same way, I feel compelled to rush into the heat of emotions. It's my conviction that there's a critical opportunity to reach and help people, early on, during the most painful and challenging times in their lives.

Here's a message that I would like to leave for all caregivers who choose to help others *during* times of crisis....

Years ago, I was warned by an esteemed psychologist never to build a clinical practice around, or specialize in working exclusively with, people in crisis. He explained how the stress of helping others, during intensely emotional times, would be too overwhelming for anyone.

Because of my belief that crises present unique and powerful opportunities for people to grow, I chose not to heed my colleague's warning. Instead, I immersed myself in helping people to live through and overcome adversity. *I chose to focus on the healing process and the hope and potential of empowering people to look beyond today and live their dreams!* This is my mission and purpose—and I've never found it to be overwhelming.

And another thought. There's nothing magical about what we say or do with people during times of crisis. In fact, it's generally not *what we say* that helps people the most, it's often *what we don't say.* Let's remember that we are not experts in solving other people's problems. No one has the right to question another person's beliefs or to tell them how they *should* feel. Instead, we should strive to become experts in helping people to find the answers within themselves. We should try to give back a sense of control that their experience seems to have taken away.

Let's support people during their crisis and help them to look beyond adversity—toward their blessings and their unique potential.

Take care of you.

Appendix B

How Do People Typically Respond During a Crisis?

There's no standard way in which we respond during a crisis. Some of us respond immediately, while others may experience a delayed reaction, sometimes months or even years down the road. Some people's reactions may last for a long period of time. For others, traumatic stress reactions are short-lived.

The reactions/responses on the pages that follow are frequently experienced *during* times of crisis. It's important to recognize that these reactions do not necessarily represent an unhealthy response. Rather, they may be viewed as *normal* responses to an *abnormal* event.

If these reactions continue to be experienced in the future and are joined by other symptoms such as recurrent distressing dreams, flashbacks, avoidance behaviors, excessive jumpiness, or panic attacks, and interfere with social, occupational or other important areas of functioning, a stress disorder may be present. Consideration should be given to consulting with a mental health professional.

Emotional Responses may include:

- shock
- denial
- dissociation
- panic
- fear
- aloneness
- hopelessness
- helplessness
- emptiness
- uncertainty
- horror
- terror
- anger
- hostility
- irritability
- sadness
- depression
- grief
- guilt

Cognitive Responses during a crisis are often reflected in:

- impaired concentration
- confusion
- disorientation
- difficulty in making a decision
- a short attention span
- suggestibility
- vulnerability
- forgetfulness
- self-blame
- blaming others
- lowered self-esteem
- thoughts of losing control
- hypervigilance
- perseverative thoughts of the traumatic event

Behavioral Responses may include:

- withdrawal
- "spacing-out"
- non-communication
- changes in speech patterns
- regressive behaviors
- erratic movements
- impulsivity
- a reluctance to abandon property
- seemingly aimless walking or pacing
- an inability to sit still
- an exaggerated startle response
- antisocial behaviors

Physiological Responses may include:

- elevated blood pressure*
- difficulty breathing*
- shock symptoms*
- chest pains*
- cardiac palpitations*
- rapid heart beat
- muscle tension and pains
- fatigue
- sleep difficulty and disturbing dreams
- fainting
- flushed face
- pale appearance
- chills
- cold clammy skin
- increased sweating
- thirst
- dizziness
- vertigo

- hyperventilation
- headaches
- grinding of teeth
- twitches
- gastrointestinal upset

These require immediate medical evaluation.

Spiritual Responses during a crisis often include:

- anger and a distancing from God
- withdrawal from attending religious services or an uncharacteristic involvement in religious community activity
- feelings that faith practice (prayers, scriptures, hymns, worship, communion) is empty and without meaning
- a questioning of one's basic beliefs and anger at clergy

Appendix C

21 Things You Can Do While You're Living Through a Crisis

1. Take immediate action to ensure your physical safety and the safety of others. If possible, remove yourself from the event/scene in order to avoid further traumatic exposure.

2. Address your acute medical needs. If you're having difficulty breathing, experiencing chest pains or palpitations, seek immediate medical attention.

3. Find a safe place that offers shelter, water, food and sanitation.

4. Become aware of how the event is affecting you (your feelings, thoughts, actions and your physical and spiritual reactions).

5. Know that your reactions are normal responses to an abnormal event. You are not "losing it" or "going crazy." It's okay not to be okay, right now.

6. Speak with your physician or healthcare provider and make him/her aware of what has happened to you.

7. Be aware of how you're holding-up when there are children around you. Children will take their cues from the adults around them.

8. Try to obtain information. Knowing the facts about what has happened will help you to keep functioning.

9. If possible, surround yourself with family and loved ones. Realize that the event is likely affecting them, too.

10. Tell your story. And allow yourself to feel. It's okay not to be okay during a traumatic experience.

11. You may experience a desire to withdraw and isolate, causing a strain on significant others. Resist the urge to shut down and retreat into your own world.

12. Traumatic stress may compromise your ability to think clearly. If you find it difficult to concentrate when someone is speaking to you, focus on the specific words they are saying and work to actively listen. Slow down the conversation and try repeating what you have just heard.

13. Don't make important decisions when you're feeling overwhelmed. Allow trusted family members or friends to assist you with necessary decision-making.

14. If stress is causing you to react physically, use controlled breathing techniques to stabilize

yourself. Take a slow deep breath by inhaling through your nose, hold your breath for five seconds and then exhale through your mouth. Upon exhalation, think the words "relax," "let go," or "I'm handling this." Repeat this process several times.

15. Realize that repetitive thinking and sleep difficulties are normal reactions. Don't fight the sleep difficulty. Try the following: eliminate caffeine for four hours prior to your bedtime, create the best sleep environment you can, consider taking a few moments before turning out the lights to write down your thoughts, thus "emptying" your mind.

16. Give yourself permission to rest, relax and engage in non-threatening activity. Read, listen to music, or consider taking a warm bath.

17. Physical exercise may help to dissipate the stress energy that has been generated by your experience. Take a walk, ride a bike, or swim.

18. Create a journal. Writing about your experience may help to expose yourself to painful thoughts and feelings and, ultimately, enable you to assimilate your experience.

19. If you find that your experience is too powerful, allow yourself the advantage of professional and/or spiritual guidance, support and education.

20. Try to maintain your schedule. Traumatic events will disrupt the sense of normalcy. We are all creatures of habit. By maintaining our routines, we can maintain a sense of control at a time when circumstances may lead us to feel a loss of control.

21. Crises present opportunities. Cultivate a mission and purpose. Seize the energy from your experience and use it to propel you to set realistic goals, make decisions and take action.

Appendix D

When It's Time for a Mental Health Professional

It's very common for people to ask when it's *necessary* to turn to a mental health professional for help. Following are four basic indicators that will help you to know if you've experienced more stress than you can handle yourself, or with the help of your friends and loved ones:

1. Persistent suicidal or homicidal thoughts

As I indicated previously, it's not unusual for us to experience thoughts of non-existence, or thoughts of harming ourselves or others, particularly during a crisis. However, if these thoughts persist, and you begin to think of *how* and *when* you may act on your thoughts, pursue professional help immediately. Don't give yourself the chance to act impulsively.

2. An inability to care for yourself

You're withdrawing from people, not eating, not sleeping, not taking care of your basic needs. Any one of these or a combination of several is an indication that it's time to pursue professional help.

3. Ongoing painful symptoms

If you're experiencing ongoing physical pain or discomfort, speak with your doctor. In the same way, if you're experiencing ongoing painful feelings, such as panic attacks or depression, speak with a mental health professional.

4. Abuse of substances

If you're turning to alcohol, tranquilizers or sleeping pills on a regular basis, or if you're using drugs to "self medicate," see a professional who can offer healthier and more effective solutions.

If you don't know of a particular mental health practitioner, turn to your doctor, a hospital or perhaps your spiritual leader, for a referral.

Acknowledgments

This book lays the foundation for a series of *It's OK Not To Be OK* publications, workshops and presentations that will ultimately help people during times of crisis.

So many people have helped me to identify my mission and purpose, and supported me both personally and professionally.

My heartfelt appreciation goes to all of you:
Stewart Gittelman, George Rogu, M.D., Nicholas Rogu, M.D., James Reilly, M.D., Joel Siev, M.D., Toba Weinstein, M.D., Steven Sugarman, M.D., Milton Agulnek, M.D., Ronnie Kastner, M.D., Charles Swersky, M.D., Alina Ciobanu, M.D., Jeffrey Mitchell, Ph.D., William Sefick, Ph.D, Chief Raymond Crawford, Raymond D. Shelton, Ph.D., Robert Fogel, M.D., Mark J. Stern, M.D.,

Howard S. Green, M.D., Glen Faber, Esq., Leslie Tayne, Esq., Robert Kronenberg, Esq., Joseph Farber, Esq., Ellenmorris Tiegerman, Ph.D., Joseph S. Volpe, Ph.D., Leonard Streim, Ph.D., Mary DiDio, D.C., Richard Garfinkel, CPA, Elizabette Cohen, DVM, MaryAnn Scafidi, Patricia McCloy, Allen Kates, Rabbi Jonathan Hecht, Ph.D., Abby G. Burton, Margaret Kenzie, Tracy Schnurr, Robert Sudaley, Bobby Senn, and publicist Michael Levine. Your friendship and support provided the fuel for my journey in writing this book.

To my parents, Carol and Edwin Lerner and to my wonderful family, Maria, Julia, Daniel and David, thank you for always being there for me.

Postscript

If I can be of help to you, please contact me. As a clinical psychologist and traumatic stress consultant, I regularly work with individuals, families, groups, organizations and corporations during times of crisis. My consultative approach is short-term. My goal is to ease emotional pain, keep people functioning and lessen the likelihood of ongoing emotional suffering. Please share with me your triumphs, questions and comments.

Mark D. Lerner, Ph.D.
Mark Lerner Associates, Inc.
P.O. Box 1315
Melville, NY 11747

MarkLernerAssociates.org
Tel. (631) 673-3513

Additional Copies

Please help me to place this book in the hands of people who are hurting. For additional copies, or if you wish to purchase copies of this publication in quantity, please contact Mark Lerner Associates, Inc.

MarkLernerAssociates.org
Tel. (631) 673-3513